Every Kid's Guide to
Handling
Disagreements

Written by
JOY BERRY

CHILDRENS PRESS ®
CHICAGO

About the Author and Publisher

Joy Berry's mission in life is to help families cope with everyday problems and to help children become competent, responsible, happy individuals. To achieve her goal, she has written over two hundred self-help books for children from birth through age twelve. Her work revolutionized children's publishing by providing families with practical, how-to, living skills information that was previously unavailable in children's books.

Joy gathered a dedicated team of experts, including psychologists, educators, child developmentalists, writers, editors, designers, and artists, to form her publishing company and to help produce her work.

The company, Living Skills Press, produces thoroughly researched books and audio-visual materials that successfully combine humor and education to teach subjects ranging from how to clean a bedroom to how to resolve problems and get along with other people.

Copyright © 1987 by Joy Berry
Living Skills Press, Sebastopol, CA
All rights reserved.
Printed in the United States of America

Managing Editor: Ellen Klarberg
Copy Editor: Kate Dickey
Contributing Editors: Libby Byers, Maureen Dryden,
Yona Flemming, Gretchen Savidge
Editorial Assistant: Sandy Passarino

Art Director: Laurie Westdahl
Design: Abigail Johnston, Laurie Westdahl
Production: Abigail Johnston, Caroline Rennard
Illustrations designed by: Bartholomew
Inker: Berenice Happe Iriks
Colorer: Berenice Happe Iriks
Composition: Curt Chelin

Each person is unique in the way he or she feels, thinks, and acts.

Because of these differences, people sometimes *disagree*.

When two or more people think the same thoughts about something, they agree.

When two or more people think different thoughts about something, they *disagree.*

Sometimes people disagree about *who* should take part in an activity.

Sometimes people disagree about *what* should be done.

Sometimes people disagree about *why* something should be done.

Sometimes people disagree about *when* something should happen.

Sometimes people disagree about *where* something should take place.

Sometimes people disagree about *how* things should be done.

When people disagree, they often experience uncomfortable feelings.

You might feel *insecure* when you disagree with another person.

You might be afraid that something bad will happen to you because you disagree.

You might feel *inferior* when you disagree with another person.

You might feel as though you are not as good as the person with whom you disagree.

You might feel *uncertain about yourself* when you disagree with another person.

You might wonder whether or not your thinking is correct.

You might also wonder whether or not you are capable of having correct thoughts.

You might feel *frustrated* when you disagree with someone.

You might feel anxious and upset.

No matter how you feel, it is important that you deal with any disagreement you might have.

Unpleasant things can happen when disagreements are not handled appropriately.

Sometimes disagreements become arguments.

Sometimes disagreements become fights.

Sometimes disagreements cause people to remain frustrated and angry. They might take their hostile feelings out on others. This is called *scapegoating*.

Scapegoating happens when a person who is involved in a disagreement hurts a person who is not involved in the disagreement.

Arguing, fighting, and scapegoating can cause people to get hurt.

Thus, it is not good when disagreements turn into arguing, fighting, and scapegoating.

You can avoid arguments, fights, and scapegoating by doing the following:

- Do not get into a discussion with another person when you are tired or in a bad mood.

- Make sure that you and everyone around you understand and agree to follow the same rules.

- Apologize and really mean it when you have been wrong.

- Remember that no one, including you, is perfect. No one is right all the time.

- Respect other people's feelings and thoughts even though they might be different from yours.

- Avoid sharing your feelings and thoughts with people who do not respect you.

You can also avoid arguments, fights, and scapegoating by resolving your disagreements. But before you can resolve your disagreements, you need to know six important facts.

Fact 1. It is OK to have disagreements.

Fact 2. It is normal for people to disagree. People who disagree are not strange or bad.

Fact 3. The thoughts of a person who disagrees are not stupid or unimportant.

Fact 4. Disagreements do not always have a right side and a wrong side.

When two people disagree, both of them can be right or both of them can be wrong.

Fact 5. It is *not* necessary for people to force themselves into thinking the same thoughts in order to resolve a disagreement.

It is OK for people to continue to have different thoughts.

Fact 6. A disagreement does not mean that the people who disagree do not like each other.

People can disagree and still like, respect, and trust each other.

Once you know the facts about disagreements, you can resolve them by following six steps.

Step 1. Define the disagreement.

Determine exactly how your thoughts differ from the other person's thoughts.

Step 2. Explore the reasons for the other person's thinking.

Encourage the other person to share his or her thoughts with you. Listen carefully to find out why the person thinks the way he or she does.

Step 3. Explain the reasons for your thinking.

Kindly and honestly tell the other person why you think the way you do.

Step 4. Research both sides of the disagreement.

Try to find out all you can about the two sides of the disagreement. To do this, you might want to consult other people and use various resource materials.

Step 5. Decide what to do about the disagreement.

There are several possible solutions to every disagreement.

You can agree with the other person.

The other person can agree with you.

Both you and the other person can compromise. You can both give in a little without either of you giving in completely.

You and the other person can agree to disagree.

Both you and the other person can change your thoughts completely.

Step 6. Do what you decide to do.

Get help if you are not able to resolve a disagreement.

Talk to a trustworthy person who will give equal consideration to both sides of the disagreement.

If necessary, allow the person to choose the best solution for the disagreement.

Disagreements will not cause problems for you or other people if you understand them and resolve them.

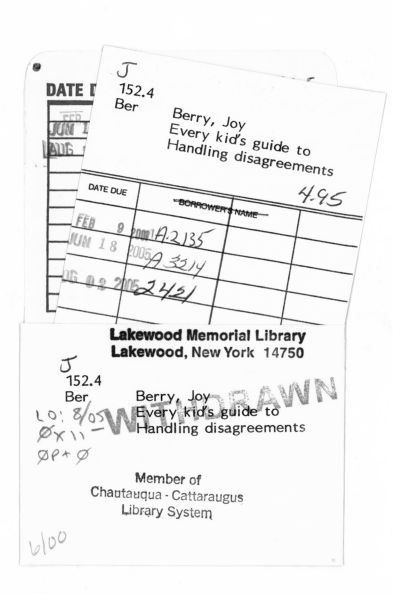